D0573765

# Opposites:

# Big and Little

Luana K. Mitten

Rourke
Publishing LLC
Vero Beach, Florida 32964

www.rourkepublishing.com

PHOTO CREDITS: © Jaroslaw Wojcik: page 3 left; © Arthur Kwiatkowski: page 3 right; © Velychko: page 5; © Alexander Shalamov: page 6, 7; © Wouter van Caspel: page 8, 9; © Ng Yin Jian: page 10, 11; © viZualStudio: page 13; © Jessica Bopp: page 14, 15; © Frank B Yuwono: page 17; © jarvis gray: page 18, 19; © Vladimirs Prusakovs: page 21; © Jelani Memory : page 22, 23; ©

Editor: Kelli Hicks

Cover design by Nicola Stratford, bdpublishing.com

Interior Design by Heather Botto

### Library of Congress Cataloging-in-Publication Data

Mitten, Luana K.
  Opposites : big and little / Luana K. Mitten.
    p. cm. -- (Concepts)
  Learning the concept of opposites through riddles and poetry.
  ISBN 978-1-60472-417-2 (hardcover)
  ISBN 978-1-60472-813-2 (softcover)
  1. English language--Synonyms and antonyms--Juvenile literature. I. Title.
  PE1591.M643 2008
  423'.1--dc22
                        2008018795

Printed in the USA

CG/CG

Rourke Publishing

www.rourkepublishing.com – rourke@rourkepublishing.com
Post Office Box 3328, Vero Beach, FL 32964

Big and little, little and big, what's the difference between big and little?

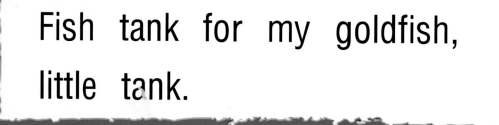

Fish tank for my goldfish,
little tank.

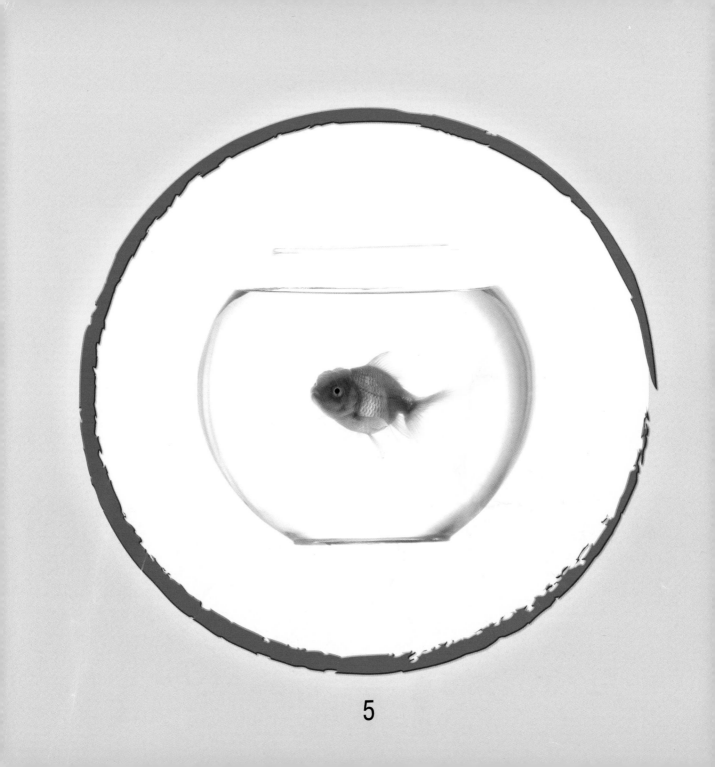

5

Fish tank for a shark,
BIG tank.

Hole for a hornet, little hole.

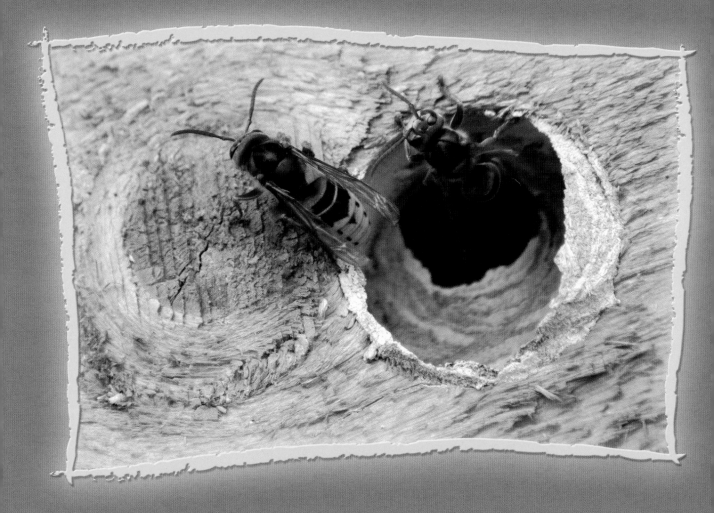

9

Hole for a rabbit, BIG hole.

Nest for a robin, little nest.

Nest for a bluebird, little nest.

Nest for an eagle, BIG nest.

Shell for a hermit crab,
little shell.

17

Shell for a sea turtle,
BIG shell.

House for a mouse,
little house.

21

House for me, BIG house!

23

# Index

## Further Reading

Child, Lauren. *Charlie and Lola's Opposites.* 2007.

Ford, Bernette. Sorrentino, Christiano. *A Big Dog: An Opposites Book,* 2008.

Falk, Laine. *Let's Talk About Opposites: Morning to Night,* 2007.

Holland, Gina. *Soft and Hard (I Know My Opposites),* 2007.

## Recommended Websites

www.abcteach.com/grammar/online/opposites1.htm

www.resources.kaboose.com/games/read1html

www.learn4good.com/kids/preschool_english_spanish_language_books.htm

## About the Author

Luana Mitten and her family live in Tampa, Florida where they like riding bikes. Luana and her husband have big bikes and her son has a little bike.